Richard Grant White

The adventures of Sir Lyon Bouse

In America during the Civil War

Richard Grant White

The adventures of Sir Lyon Bouse
In America during the Civil War

ISBN/EAN: 9783337119850

Printed in Europe, USA, Canada, Australia, Japan

Cover: Foto ©ninafisch / pixelio.de

More available books at **www.hansebooks.com**

THE ADVENTURES

OF

SIR LYON BOUSE, BART.,

IN AMERICA,

DURING THE CIVIL WAR.

Being Extracts from his Diary.

NEW YORK:

THE AMERICAN NEWS COMPANY,

GENERAL AGENTS.

1867.

CAMBRIDGE:

STEREOTYPED AND PRINTED BY

JOHN WILSON AND SON.

THE ADVENTURES

OF

SIR LYON BOUSE, BART.

———•———

CHAPTER I.

ARRIVAL IN NEW YORK. — MOB ON THE PIER. — STRANGE
MILITARY CELEBRATION. — UNPREJUDICED OPINION OF THE
WAR AND THE AMERICAN PEOPLE. — NEITHER WILD BEASTS
NOR SMALL GAME IN THE PARK. — COLD RECEPTION AT A
HOTEL.

I ARRIVED in New York on the 25th of
November, 1861. Directly I landed I saw a
mob. Just as I had expected. They were armed
with whips, and wore brass badges with numbers
— signs of a secret association, I suppose — upon
their hats. They shouted and yelled at us as we
came off the ship; thus affording me evidence,
before I was well ashore, of the American hatred
of every thing British.

As these people did not, however, seem disposed to actual violence, and as I saw something
resembling a policeman hard by, I ventured upon
the pier with my luggage, when they rushed at
me and it, vociferating so loudly, that I could not
understand a word; but I discovered, to my sur-

prise, that many of these Americans spoke with a very strong Irish accent, and that they wished, not to kill me, but to take me and my luggage to my hotel. I asked the policeman if I could trust myself to them. I must say that he treated the subject with great indifference, and even seemed to be somewhat amused at it, which I thought unbecoming; but as he told me that it would be all right if I would look sharp, and as he was an official person, I committed myself and my portmanteaus to one of these fellows, selecting him who appeared to be the quietest and best-natured. I doubted very much his assertion, that he had a hackney coach, or, as he called it, a carriage, at hand, and followed him very warily. But what he said proved true; and, indeed, I was astonished at the handsomeness of both his coach and his horses. The equipage was certainly a most extraordinary one for such a country as America. How it got here, to be sure, I can't imagine.

As I passed up the Broadway, my coachman turned suddenly into a side street. I saw that he was compelled to do so by the march of a column of troops down the Broadway; and as it was evidently a holiday turn-out, I asked him what was the occasion of this parade. The rattle of the coach prevented me from hearing all of his reply. I could only distinguish, "twinty-fifth — avvaccyation — British airmy — sillybrate." But this was enough. Was there ever such an extraordinary people as this! — to celebrate, by a mili-

tary parade, the day on which they were compelled to evacuate their own city by the British
army!

Looking forward a little, I may say that this
incident may be regarded as an example of the
manners and customs and public doings of the
Americans. They do exactly different to what
we do at home. What wonder, then, that they
are so ridiculous and so offensive!

I have come here to make observations for my
own satisfaction, and to look after some stock
which pays me only six and three-quarters per
cent, whereas I was induced to buy it on the representation that it paid seven per cent; the only
excuse given for this villanous deception being,
that the country is involved in civil war. What
business, then, had they to engage in civil war,
and reduce the interest on my stock, when the
interests of humanity and civilization required
that the government should be broken up! But,
although I have come here solely for private pur-
poses, I do not see why my friends should not
have the benefit of such observations as I shall jot
down in my note-book. In one respect, they will
be valuable: they will be written in that spirit of
fairness and candor which generally distinguishes
British writers; for I am a man entirely without
prejudice. Of course, I have all the feelings
which it is proper and correct for a Briton to
have. I like every thing that is British; but this
is no more than every true-born Briton is bound

to do; and I am proud to own that I hate
Yankees from the bottom of my heart. I will
also add, that, this being my first visit to America,
I shall have the advantage of presenting a fresh
and altogether unbiassed view of affairs in this
country; for, until I came here, I had the good
fortune never to have seen a Yankee in my life.

To resume my narrative. After I had been
driven a short distance up the Broadway, my
coachman turned round, and said, "We're comin'
to the Pairk, yer honor." This was interesting
information. I had prudently taken my rifle,
loaded, though in its leather case, into the coach
for self-defence if I should meet with highway-
men, or encounter the mobs which roam the
streets here; and, on receiving this intimation, I
took out the weapon, hoping for a chance shot at
a grisly bear, or at least a buffalo, as we drove
past. Imagine my disgust at finding that what
is called the "Park" here, is a small triangular
space containing some public buildings, and now
some temporary barracks. This is another example of the untrustworthiness of this people.
In a park, and especially in *the* park, of course
one expects to find specimens of the wild game
peculiar to the country in which one is travelling;
but here it is filled with citizens, soldiers, and
public buildings; and, although the former are
certainly fair game,[1] yet, until the resources of

[1] I hope my readers will not miss the point of my remark.
I don't mean that the Yankees are really *game* like pheasants

the pen are exhausted upon them, it is hardly fair to use the rifle.

When my cabman deposited me at my hotel, I remonstrated with him upon the deception to which he had been a party. He replied, "Oh! is it the shootin' yer afther? Well, thin, yer honor 'll be mainin' the Cinthral Pairk that's out o' town. That's three miles long, an' quite wild-like. May be ye 'll get a shot at a buffalo there?" At the same time he winked tremendously at the porter who took my luggage, and who grinned back in a most disrespectful manner.

I notice this as a specimen of the disgustingly free and easy manners of the lower orders in this country. I also here denounce them once for all, as the most deceitful of human creatures. For, on my going to the Central Park, rifle in hand, I was turned back by a policeman, whom I did not exactly wish to shoot, and told that no guns were allowed to pass the gates. This fellow had also the impudence to laugh in the most disgusting manner. I also here solemnly protest that I have not seen either a bear or a buffalo since my arrival at New York. So utterly may one find one's reasonable expectations disappointed in this execrable country.

I was soon installed in my hotel with some tolerable approach to comfort; that is, as nearly as

and partridges. I use the word in a double sense, and with a joke which I must confess is rather hard upon these Americans. — L. B.

one can be comfortable, by being left entirely to take care of one's self.   For the landlord did not come to welcome me, or, indeed, come near me ; neither did boots, nor the chambermaid.   In fact, no one took the slightest notice of me whatever, beyond handing me a brass key which had not been previously warmed, and directing the porter to take my luggage to my room.

Such treatment of an English baronet naturally aroused my resentment, and I thought of bringing the matter to the attention of Lord Lyons, with a demand, either for the prompt notice of the matter, in some way, by the American Government, and an ample apology, or the immediate despatch of a British fleet of observation to these waters, to enforce that respect to British subjects which belongs to them in virtue of their birth. But, before I could conveniently take this step to vindicate British honor, I discovered that the neglect which I experienced was but the usual custom among this inhospitable, undiscriminating, low-bred people.

How different such a reception from that which the traveller meets, for instance, at the Bull's Head (a bull's head *vert* is the Bouse crest), in the village of Tawroston, near my own estate ! — the landlord bowing and smiling, and rubbing his hands, and exclaiming with subdued ardor, "Welcome, Sir Lyon! welcome to the Bull's Head !" and the helpers and waiters ready ; some looking after one's luggage ; one going to light a fire in the parlor; chambermaid hurrying off to dust and "tidy up," and see that well-aired sheets are on the bed; and, in fact, the whole household seeming to overflow with simple, hearty, unaffected welcome, and to be agog with readiness to serve.

I have noticed with pain that this charming old custom is not kept up, even in England, as it should be; that, in fact, it exists nowhere in perfection but at the Bull's Head; and that, the farther one gets from Tawroston, the greater one discovers to be the degeneracy in this particular. The same falling-off has been noticed more or less by several of my friends, country gentlemen of large estate and much influence in their counties, and whose opinion is therefore not to be lightly disputed. They tell me, that, the nearer they get to London or Liverpool, the more they remark this neglect of proper respect; and they all attribute it to the deleterious influence of democracy upon those cities through their commerce with this country. For, as to the Americans, the ill-bred clowns do not know, nor did they ever know, any thing of the delightful custom. However, thanks to Commodore Wilkes, we may soon have the opportunity of teaching them better manners (for of course they won't give up the Confederate commissioners); though it is to be doubted whether they will ever attain that ease and grace, and that consideration for the feelings of others, by which the true Briton is distinguished all over the world.

I am determined to be candid; and I therefore frankly admit, that, to my great surprise, I found that the sheets upon my bed were pretty clean; and indeed, on a close examination, I could not discover sufficient evidence to justify a complaint that they had been slept in by any other person since they came from the laundry. I also, in the same spirit of candor, unhesitatingly state that there was a fair supply of clean towels in my room, and that I had fresh ones always when I wanted them, and that there was plenty of water for washing. I accounted for this by the necessity of consulting the tastes and habits of my countrymen, so many of whom are compelled to visit America. Yet there must, I think, have sprung up a customary use of water among persons indigenous to the soil; for, in a corner of my room, there was a strange triangular contrivance with a marble top, consisting partly of a fixed bowl, into which water ran from a faucet, though with a very confusing splutter and splash, — to say nothing of the impropriety of asking a gentleman to draw water for himself, instead of having servants at call to bring it. This machine plainly indicated, I thought, the existence of some sort of attempt at an aqueduct in the vicinity.

After these good-natured, and, I may say, highly laudatory admissions on my part, the Americans cannot deny the fairness of spirit, the lack of prejudice, or, I fancy, the keenness of penetration, which I bring to the ungrateful and

disgusting task of examining their manners, customs, and "institootions." I would call to their
attention, as applicable to my case, a passage in
one of the works of our great British bard, some
copies of whose dramas must have reached this
country : —

> " nothing extenuate,
> Nor aught set down in malice," —

a passage, by the way, upon the discovery of
which, and its applicability to circumstances like
the present, I think I may justly pride myself.
This, then, is the generous mood in which I
undertake my loathsome labors.

CHAPTER II.

AFTER I had performed the duties of the toilet with that thoroughness which is so distinctively English, I rang, and, on the appearance of the waiter, said, " Send me the landlord."

The fellow stood staring with open mouth a moment, and then said, " Is it Misther C—— ye want ? "

" How should I know whether it's Mr. This or Mr. That ? What's his name to me, or what's it to me whether he has any name ? Attend to your business, and send me the landlord, I say."

The fellow went out, and after a long time, just as I was about to ring again, there was a knock at the door, and a nondescript sort of person entered (most persons in America are nondescript), who asked me what he could do for me. " Are you the landlord ? " I asked. No, he was not. " Are you the head-waiter ? " No, nor the head-waiter : he was a clerk. " Then, what the devil, sir, if you're not the landlord or the head-

waiter, are you doing in my room? Send me the
landlord. I want to know what I can have for
luncheon." He replied that the Hon. Mr. C——
was the landlord — he called it. the proprietor
— of the hotel, and that he was attending the
legislature, — which is some sort of thing like a
parliament that they have here somewhere; and
adding, with the most unbecoming curtness, that
I should find luncheon in the dining-room, and
that the waiters would bring me any thing I
wanted, he had the impudence to coolly turn
upon his heel and go out without another word,
or waiting to hear what I might have to say. A
landlord at the legislature, instead of being ready
at call to look after the comfort of his guests, and
leaving a clerk to tell a baronet that he would
find luncheon in the dining-room! Plainly, the
people in this country don't know their places.
I must teach them.

Immediately I entered the dining-room, I saw
that I should probably have the good fortune of
taking luncheon quite alone, attended by three
waiters. I was not disappointed. A person entered the room, indeed, while I was at table, and
took a seat, but not within any disrespectful or
disagreeable propinquity. Of course I was not
going to ruin my digestion and get my mouth
out of taste by eating any of their nasty American messes, without knowing any thing about
them; and, as the landlord was not there to tell
me what I could have, and give the proper expla-

nations, I desired one of the waiters to bring me some ship's-biscuit and a bottle of Alsop's ale from my own hamper which was up-stairs in my room. But he answered, that they had those ready at hand. I was surprised, of course; but, on reflecting again that New York was a seaport in direct communication with London and Liverpool, I saw in a moment how this happened, and so was well pleased to save my stores for use in places less fortunately situated.

After I had despatched my ale and biscuits, (which I confess with pleasure had the real English flavor), much gratified with this my first experience in observing the manners and modes of life of the Americans, I sallied out to continue my observations, having taken the precaution to provide myself with some American money. So then I thought I would go and see my friend A——, a jolly Yorkshireman, who came over in the ship with me, and who had gone to private lodgings.

After inquiring my way to his street, — numbered something less than a thousand, — I hailed an omnibus. To my surprise and disgust, there was no conductor. A miserable arrangement this, and not at all like what we have at home, where one is always sure to find a person in this situation who is obliged to know his place, and to whom one can make those reasonable complaints for which there is always so much cause, without the unpleasantness of being answered back. Instead of finding this very useful person ready to open

the door of the vehicle, I saw the door open mys-
teriously of itself as I approached it, and shut to
with a sharp bang after I had entered. This was
a very astonishing process. I had heard something of the ingenuity of the Americans in me-
chanical invention, but never imagined any thing
so extraordinary as this. I noticed a leathern
strap running along the top of the omnibus inside,
toward the driver's seat, which, it occurred to
me, might possibly have some connection with
this phenomenon.

Mem. To investigate the character of this
remarkable contrivance, and take a description,
with diagrams, back to Tawroston with me. It
may be usefully applied to the doors at Bouse
Hall, and relieve one of the necessity of ringing
to have the door shut.

Soon after I had taken my seat, the man who
sat next to me, and whom, it is needless to say,
I had never seen before, had the impudence to
turn to me and tell me that it was a very fine
morning; and, while I was wondering at the
extraordinary customs of this semi-barbarous people, he had the effrontery to add, that he hoped
we should have a continuation of fine weather for
the sake of the army. Of course I took no notice
of him whatever. What business had he to ob-
trude his judgment of the weather on me, or his
hopes? And, as to his army, what was it to me
if the blackguards all rotted in a heap? The
sooner the better, perhaps; for then this ridicu-

lous, savage, vulgar war might stop, and the deficient quarter per cent on my stock be paid.

While I was thinking over this unpleasant experience, and devising measures to protect myself against its recurrence during my future travels here, there was a sudden and dreadful pounding on the top of the omnibus; but no one seemed to notice it. After a few minutes, it was heard again, with increased vigor. I looked up, and at my fellow-passengers inquiringly, and found that they were also looking at me inquiringly. But, as the pounding soon ceased, I fell again into the pleasant train of reflections to which the soothing influence of Alsop's ale is so favorable, when, all at once, the pounding broke out again with such fury, that it seemed to me as if the top of the omnibus must come in. I looked round again, and again found all my companions looking at me, evidently very much interested to know what my opinion was of this remarkable occurrence. I was about to express my annoyance and indignation in proper terms, when one of them said to me, —

"Strannger, I rayther guess as haow de gemman wants yeour farr afore totein yeouw any furder."

"The gentleman? What gentleman?"

"Wahl, th' driver; 'n I reckon he'd like to hev yeou fork over pooty c'nsidubble darn'd quick. Yes, sar."[1]

---

[1] The American editor of this diary allows this representation of the dialect spoken in this country to appear as it is

I will remark here, in passing, once for all, that this is the style of speech and manners which is found in all classes all over this country, except certain people who seem to be natives, and who yet, unaccountably, talk and behave like English gentleman of average cultivation; but of course no one comes to America to see or write about them.

But I resume my story. I replied, "Very well, if the driver wants my fare, why don't he come and get it? How can I give it to him?"

"Up thar;" pointing to a small round hole in the front of the top of the omnibus.

I took out my fare, which I had previously found to be six cents (equal to about three pence sterling), and was going to push it up through the hole, when one of the passengers who sat nearer the front (it will hardly be believed), put out his hand with the evident intention of taking my money from me. Such a barefaced attempt at

---

written in the author's manuscript. It certainly has the merit of being quite like that which has been given by Sir Lyon's predecessors. Its only fault is, that being composed of a mixture, in about equal parts, of the dialects of the Southern negro, the rustic Yankee, and the Western backwoodsman, it consequently was never heard here from the lips of any human being, or anywhere except from the Yankee of the British stage. In subsequent passages, for the convenience of readers on this side of the water, the speech of the various personages introduced will be conformed as much as possible to what it would appear that the author must have heard. This is the only liberty that will be taken with the text of the veracious record of this intelligent and unprejudiced observer.

robbery I never saw or heard of before. Yet
what might I not have expected in America!
My experience about my stock might have taught
me. But I was not to be taken off my guard. I
clutched my money tightly, and asked him what
he meant by such ruffianly conduct. He had the
audacity to ask my pardon, and to say that he
only meant to save me some trouble. But I was
not to be taken in by any such palaver, and was
about to tell him that he was a d——d repudiating
Yankee, when, as I stood with my head bent
down, the omnibus started off at a quick pace
over the ice-blocked street, which caused such a
frightful jolting, that my hat was crushed over
my eyes, and I quickly thrown down in a sitting
posture upon the floor of the infernal machine
into which I had been entrapped. Of course this
was a concerted plan between the driver and
the robbers inside; but I clutched my six cents
closely in one hand, and put the other upon my
pocket-book. I felt — for, from the condition of
my head, I could not see — hands upon me which
lifted me up; but I broke from them, and, tear-
ing off my hat, resumed my seat for a moment.
After casting a withering glance at this pretty
specimen assemblage of Americans, I left the
omnibus precipitately, and paid the driver outside,
giving him, at the same time, a piece of my mind,
for which the scoundrel reviled me as long as he
was in sight. I should not omit saying that this
scandalous occurrence was deemed a particularly

good joke by the thieves among whom I had fallen, all of whom drove off on the broad grin.

Of course I resolved that I would never enter an American omnibus again. But I afterward discovered a reason for the adoption of this custom of payment through a hole, in addition to the facilities which it affords for robbery. It is this. America, being without nobility and gentry, there are therefore, of course, no distinctions in society. So the young ladies of the wealthiest and best-educated families, (according to such education as there is here), frequently choose their lovers from among the omnibus-drivers; and their usual mode of expressing a tender preference for any particular Jehu is to kiss his hand as he puts it through the hole in question for the fare. This affords them an opportunity to bestow the coveted and significant caress very conveniently, and without attracting too much attention. Sometimes, in this way, one driver will have offers from half a dozen of the prettiest and richest girls in the city.

There is also another custom, of an equally tender nature, brought into vogue by this mode of payment. As the drivers take the fares while the omnibus is in motion, of course, having the reins in one hand, they have only one at liberty with which to handle the money. They supply the deficiency by putting the silver and the copper into their mouths as they make change; and then they hand it, adhering well together, through the hole. The young lady who is enamored of one of these fortunate whips, takes the money and puts it between her pretty lips for a moment, and thus is enabled slyly to secure a sort of kiss from the object of her regard, without being openly put to the blush. This custom is universal. It accounts for the fact, that, in America, omnibus-drivers always marry the daughters of millionnaires.

CHAPTER III.

MISCELLANEOUS REFLECTIONS. — DISAPPOINTMENT AT BREAK-
FAST. — INCOMPREHENSIBLE BEHAVIOR OF THE GUESTS. —
TWO REAL AMERICANS. — PROOF OF THE BEASTLY NATURE
OF THE AMERICAN PEOPLE. — NEW-YORK HERALDRY. — THE
BEND SINISTER. — REASONS FOR ITS PREVALENCE. — FULL
DRESS IN THE MORNING. — ANONYMA IN BROADWAY. — A
PUZZLING QUESTION.

HAVING dined and passed my first evening
in America with my Yorkshire friend, —
talking, the reader may be sure, with pride of
the glories of old England, and regret at being
brought into this half-civilized place by the ras-
cality of its inhabitants, who, in the most dis-
honorable manner, have half-ruined themselves
by this silly, disgusting war just after I had put
some thousands of pounds into their stocks, — I
rose this morning not having a very clear idea of
where I was. But I soon discovered; and, on
opening the shutters, I saw that it was not a London November day upon which I looked.

It must be confessed that they do have a very
fine sun in this country; but I have no doubt,
that, if we could only contrive some method of
consuming our own fog and smoke at home, the
sun would be much better in England.

I rang for hot water, and was surprised to find how quickly it was brought me. I therefore ventured to ask for soda-water. "Yes, sir; all right, sir," said the waiter, and actually, in a few minutes, he fetched it. I asked when I could have my breakfast. "Breakfast from seven to eleven, sir" was the answer. I was about to order it up, when I remembered reading yesterday some rules stuck on the door of my chamber, and that one of them was, that all meals served in rooms would be charged extra.

Yes, these people actually undertook to give me bed and board for three dollars a day; and, when I come to look into the matter, I find that I am to pay five dollars a day extra for my sitting-room, and that, unless I choose to eat with a mob of a hundred and fifty Yankees, I am to pay double for every thing I eat!

I complained about this at the office; and they had the impudence to answer, "Of course, sir, you can't expect us to furnish private rooms and private tables to our guests at the same price as when they live in common! We could not afford it. We should be ruined directly. Every guest would have his private table. And people in this country know that we can accommodate them as we do at the price we ask only upon the principle of combination." A pretty answer! What have I to do with their disgusting gregarious customs! But remembering that I was in a wilderness, where one must not expect to be comfortable as one is at home, and remembering also the deficiency in interest on my stock, I concluded to save my two or three guineas a day, and breakfast and dine at the *table d' hote*, and do without a private sitting-room.

I am very glad, too, that I did not bring Jenkins, my valet. True, I miss his services while dressing; but he is a treasure, and being very well behaved, (having caught some of the manner of the persons about whom he has been,) I was afraid that he might be snapped up by some half-savage heiress here; and what I learned about the omnibus-drivers makes me very glad of my decision to continue him on half wages, with his time to himself, till I return.

Things did not go at breakfast quite as I thought I had reason to expect. Instead of two or three hundred voracious people eating all at once, there were only a score or so at a time; for, as some sat down to table, others rose and went out. The breakfast was as uninteresting as possible,—no spitting, no laying of quids of tobacco on the cloth, no man putting his heels upon the table, everybody chatting quietly or reading newspapers, and, in fact, nothing at all doing to interest the traveller.

The people looked a little different to what they do at home; and, in particular, I noticed that the men and women who had reached middle age had not that pleasing and dignified rotundity of form and richness of complexion, which, I have observed, produces so agreeable an impression at Tawroston; (I mean, of course, in the person of my friend Sir Hardbottle Grindstone;) still I saw very plainly that they were not real Americans. I therefore gave my attention to breakfast, which, I candidly confess, I did not find quite so bad as might have been reasonably expected.

I had, however, the satisfaction of seeing one man chop up two eggs in a goblet, and another rise from the table chewing his last mouthful, and pick his teeth with a huge pearl-handled pocket-knife before he got to the door. I felt sure that these must be real Americans, and that the latter was a man of consequence among the natives; for, although his linen was soiled, he was dressed in fine black broadcloth, and wore a heavy gold chain across his black satin waistcoat, and a large diamond ring on the little finger of his left hand.

On inquiry at the office, I found, to my great satisfaction, that I was right. He came from Maine, where he was a lumberman, as they call a wood-cutter here, and had gone to California, and made a fortune as a digger. As this was as long ago as 1850, he was regarded as one of the solid old millionnaires of New York; and it was expected that he would found a professorship of good manners at Columbia College, and attain the eclat of a hero by going to Europe in his own vessel in search of social consideration.

My success in detecting a real American at sight of course not only gratified me, but begot in me a modest confidence in my own judgment.

After breakfast, I went out for a·walk. I had hardly crossed two streets before I found striking and unmistakable evidence of the bestial nature of the Americans, which they themselves boast in their saying that they are "half horse, half alligator." For there, upon the curbstones and dead-walls all around, was posted the confession, "WE ALL USE KELLINGER'S LINIMENT." Now, this Kellinger's Liniment, as I had seen by my newspaper at breakfast, is an ointment *for horses.* It is very clear, then, from this naïve confession, made in public after the fashion of the people, that the real Americans are what they claim to be, half horse at least, if not half alligator. I made a memorandum to investigate as to the alligator half, and may find it out by discovering some other remedy in common use.

Noticed on my walk many houses with shields carved in the stone over the doors, which I regarded with mingled scorn for the presumption of these people in using shields, and pleasure at the decadence of democracy, of which they are unmistakable evidence. I also observed with surprise that most of these shields displayed the bend sinister, for which I was quite at loss to account, especially as the shields with this bearing would sometimes be upon a dozen or twenty houses together.

It was a remarkable circumstance, too, that these houses in rows were exactly alike. And sometimes a long row in one street would be so like a row in a street that I had just passed, that I could not distinguish the streets from each other, more than the houses.

I afterward learned that the houses are not only thus alike externally, but that internally their structure is identical, and that even the locks on the front doors of a row are all alike, so that one latch-key will open them all. This similarity leads to many mistakes of a peculiar nature, which, in any other country but the States, would soon cause a change to be made in the style of domestic architecture. For a gentleman going home late is often, it will readily be believed, quite unable to tell his own home from his neighbor's. He cannot say with the Scotch poet, —

> " This is no my ain house,
> I ken by the bigging o't; "

for the building of it is no different from that of a dozen or two in the same row. His latch-key lets him in; the houses are just alike inside, and furnished exactly alike. The way up stairs is just what it is at his own house, and, should it so happen that the other gude mon is also expected home, his entrance will create no alarm; and there is no telling what may happen before he discovers that he is in the wrong house.

When I learned all this, the propriety of the

shields with the bar sinister upon these houses
was of course manifest. This explained also
why the shields are put upon the houses when
they are first built, and it is not known who were
to be their tenants. It is mere foresight of what
seems to be regarded as inevitable.

In the course of my walk, I met no less than
three people in evening dress, two men in black
dress coats and trousers, and a woman in a rather
low silk dress with short sleeves, with only a sleazy
lace shawl over her shoulders. She seemed a
very pleasant and agreeable person indeed. My
expectations are thus in one point confirmed. It
is plain that the Americans often go about in full
dress in the morning. I wondered what was the
reason of this common custom, and how it had
come to be thus generally adopted.

A little reflection soon showed me how it was.
The Americans being very fond of gay society,
and at the same time always in a hurry, go to
parties in the evening, come home very late at
night, go to bed in their clothes, and get up
ready dressed in the morning, — a great saving
of time and trouble. But the clothes suffer. The
black coats become rusty, the female finery,
which in any case is not well suited to the day-
light, soiled and rumpled, and the light gloves,
dingy.

Yet it is very remarkable, as I noticed after-
wards, that the ladies at my hotel invariably come
to dinner with dresses high to the throat and

down to the wrists. I must also say that I never
can get from any one of them an encouragement
to open an acquaintance with her by some light
and graceful persiflage, a chuck under the chin,
or any of those little attentions by which a man
of position always ought to show his affability
and gallantry to the native women of a place
through which he is travelling. Whereas, on the
contrary, the woman in the lace shawl, whom I
met this morning, very plainly showed me indica-
tions of a willingness to be pleased with any
attention by which I might think proper to distinguish her. Such is the singular and unaccountable difference of costume and capriciousness in
manners among this extraordinary and peculiar
people.

I had been told by a fellow-traveller whose
acquaintance I made on my voyage out, that
the most elegant and distinguished as well as the
most beautiful women whom you meet in the
Broadway are the Anonymas, — the pretty horse-
breakers, as they are called in London. This did
not agree entirely with my previous impressions
with regard to the country, — that every thing is
just exactly different to what it is at home. But
of course a native would know better than I.
Therefore this morning, when I saw a young
woman so elegant, so distinguished, and so beautiful that there could be no doubt whatever
as to her anonymousness, I stepped up and
spoke to her, only, I assure my readers, for the

purpose of investigating, as a stranger and a tourist, the manners and customs of the country in this as in other particulars.

To my surprise, she did not reply, but started, blushed, and hurried on. But, supposing that very naturally she might be abashed by being addressed by a man of my rank and position, I repeated my salutation in the most encouraging manner. But she screamed a little scream as she ran forward to a gentleman who was approaching, crying out to him, "O Charles!" and in a moment the villain struck at me, and just touched me under the ear; but I, in drawing back from his blow, — I assure my readers for no other reason, — fell off the curb-stone into the kennel.

I did not lose my self-possession a moment; and, seeing at once that this was another contrivance of this "smart" and swindling people to rob me, I clapped my hand upon my pocket, and shouted, "Police, police! Send me a policeman, if there is such a thing in this infernal country!" A crowd instantly gathered around, and a tremendous fellow in a uniform of blue with gold buttons, and a cap, and who was very plainly, I thought, an officer in their army, stepped up and said, "I saw this, sir, and you'd better be quiet, and go about your business as quickly as possible. You didn't actually assault the lady; and as the gentleman has gone off with her, and very plainly don't want to appear against you, I shan't arrest you.

But you may thank him that I don't take you to the station-house."

So it was a policeman, and this is the way things are managed in this country. Women who are no better than they should be decoy gentlemen into the clutches of their pals to have them robbed; and when they fail, owing to the presence of mind of their intended victim, there is a policeman disguised in an officer's uniform, ready at hand to step up and cover their retreat. Was there ever such another country or such another people in the world?

I shall stop here a few days, so that I may understand the people; for as the Americans live in public, (and every Englishman knows that they do,) if you see the hotels and the theatres, and the people in the streets and on the railways, you have seen the country, except, of course, the prairies and the buffaloes. I mean to look at it thoroughly and candidly. As all Americans live in hotels, of course the wealthiest men, and those of most cultivation and highest social position, must live in the largest and finest hotels; and, as mine is one of the largest and finest, I shall look sharp there for specimens of the best breeding and education in the country.

One thing puzzled me very much this morning. Americans live in public and chiefly at hotels, as I have remarked already; but yet, in my walk in the quiet cross-streets, I saw long rows of houses stretching away into the distance, having an air singularly like that of private houses; and, indeed, they were plainly small and self-contained dwelling-houses. I noticed yesterday, when I went up town to visit my Yorkshire friend A——, that I passed through street after street of these houses, brown stone and brick; a solid square mile on each side I went through, I am sure.

Now, what can the Americans want with all these houses? In any other country, we should know that private families lived in them, and that, in England, each one of them was at once a castle and a home for brave, warm hearts to dwell in. But in a country where the people have no idea of home or of privacy, and live in huge, staring hotels, in boarding-houses, in the saloons of steamboats, and in railway cars, the existence of these square miles of private-looking houses is most unaccountable. I am told that in various towns, cities, and villages scattered over the country, the same remarkable fact is to be noticed. What an extraordinary, singular, and altogether unsatisfactory people the Americans are, to be sure! I must devote myself to the reconciliation of this singular inconsistency, with the facts as they are conclusively established upon British authority; than which, I need hardly say, there cannot be better.

CHAPTER IV.

MR. BARNUM AND HIS MUSEUM. — A REPRESENTATIVE MAN AND A REPRESENTATIVE INSTITUTION. — THE LECTURE-ROOM. — WOMEN'S RIGHTS MOVEMENT. — ENCOUNTER WITH MR. BARNUM. — INTRODUCTION TO A GIANTESS.

MR. BARNUM, I take it, is the representative man, and his museum is the representative "institootion" of this country. Should any Yankee be captious and dishonest enough to dispute this assertion, I shall content myself with referring him to the name of this celebrated establishment, — Barnum's *American* Museum. And I should like to know, if the British Museum is to be taken as an index of the state of civilization in Great Britain, why the American Museum is not to be looked upon in a similar light as regards America? And, if not, I ask again why the government don't disavow the place, and cause it to be shut up until the name is changed? The majority governs in this country; therefore the will of the majority is the government; and, if the majority did not consent that Mr. Barnum should set his place up as "*The American* Museum," of course he could not do it. Besides, has not this ingenious gentleman made one fortune by humbug, according to his own confession, and another by wooden clocks? What then is lacking to complete his national representative character?

The chief objects of popular and scientific interest in America may therefore be safely pronounced to be giants, fat women, white whales, dwarfs, hippopotami, and negroes of the Wotisitt tribe.[1] A lecture-room is attached to the museum, as might be expected. The lectures are altogether upon moral subjects. The advance of the Woman's Rights movement in this country is shown by the fact that the lecturers are mostly women who wear the Bloomer costume without the trousers. The lectures are sometimes delivered to the sound of music; and the lecturers adopt a peculiar style of gesture, often standing upon one foot and gesticulating with the other. It is said to be very impressive. It gives me pleasure to record one admirable peculiarity of this moral lecture-room : Mr. Barnum guarantees the strict virtue of all ladies who are its habitual attendants.

I visited Barnum's Museum myself, but did not remain there long. A giant and giantess were on exhibition, and almost the first object that met my eyes after I had got well into the place was the giant, — a very large man indeed, I frankly

---

[1] This name has been corrupted by the Americans, who corrupt every thing, even the names of their own tribes, into "What is it?" — L. B.

confess, — head and shoulders taller than any of
the Guards; and a very fine figure of a man he
looked as he walked about in a cavalry uniform,
with a helmet upon his head. But he was not
an American; and as I had heard that the
giantess, who was said to be taller than the giant,
was an American, in fact a "Down-East" Yankee,
and as I doubted very much the ability of New
England to produce any thing gigantic, except
brag and swindles, I was anxious to see her.
But, when I inquired for her, I was told that she
was not then to be seen, as she had retired for a
short time to rest. Here was another swindle, to
begin with. This man Barnum advertised his
giantess as to be seen; I paid my money, and,
when I asked to see her, she was *not* to be seen.
I began to say very plainly what I thought of
such an imposition; but the people around me,
to my surprise, although they gathered near
and listened, did not back me, or show much
sympathy.

Presently a portly, curly-haired man in black
approached, and I heard some one say, "There
comes Mr. Barnum himself." He came up and
asked what was the matter; adding, in the smooth-
est manner, that he hoped nothing had happened
to dissatisfy the patrons of his establishment. I
told him that I wanted to see the giantess I had
paid to see, and that she was not there. "Well,"
he said, "I'm sorry she isn't here. But she's ben
here all the morning; and we hev to be a little

careful and easy with our giants. Giants ain't
quite up to so much exhibition work, standin'
round an' like, as people that isn't giants. An'
so we spell 'em, particularly the lady giants.
[What could he mean by spelling giants?] Our
Belgian friend here'll have to go and take a rest
pretty soon, and then the lady'll come out." The
reader may be sure that I was not to be put off
with any such chaff as this; and I told the man
in pretty plain terms what I thought of his scoun-
drelly behavior, which, I added, was just what
might be expected from a clock-making Yankee.
To my surprise, he offered no apology, nor did
he get angry; but said to my very face, that,
although he did not undertake to enforce good
manners in his establishment, he always expected
them, and from Yankees he always had them,
whether they made clocks or not. Then, taking
out a quarter of a dollar, he had the impudence
to offer it to me, and to say, that, as I was dissat-
isfied, he would be pleased if I would take my
money and go. But I was determined not to be
put off in this manner; and so I told him that I
didn't want my money back, and wouldn't take it.
I wanted to see the giantess, and that I should be
satisfied with nothing less. He looked at me a
moment with a queer expression in his eyes,
which I remember having seen in the eyes of
many of his countrymen afterward, and said,
" So you must see the giantess, must you?"—
" Yes, of course I must."—" Well, then," taking

me aside a little, "I think I shall hev to give you a private interview, if that'll suit." I was pleased to find that a little becoming self-assertion, and taking a decided stand, had produced a proper effect: a private exhibition was, of course, most agreeable to me.

Mr. Barnum disappeared for a few minutes, and, when he returned, he slipped his arm very coolly into mine, and led me off to a side room. As we entered, he asked me my name, and, on learning it, said, "Oh! I know you very well, sir, by reputation, although I have never had the pleasure of meeting you before." This was also gratifying. [P.S. It was gratifying at the time, but I have since discovered that this is the remark made in this country by every man to every other man on first making his acquaintance. Every man is supposed to be so far "one of our most eminent citizens" as to have a reputation with which all those who meet him, and who wish to be polite, must profess to be familiar.] Mr. Barnum led me up to a sofa where the giantess was sitting. I saw a huge, moony face, above a pair of monstrous shoulders, and a mass of female drapery. The face was on a level with my own, although I was standing. "Miss Condor," said Mr. B., with the formality of a master of ceremonies, "allow me to introduce Sir Lyon Bouse, of England; Sir Lyon Bouse, Miss Condor." I was taken very much aback. To have a private view of a curiosity is one thing, and is an attention quite suitable to one's reasonable expectations; but to be *introduced* to a giantess!— that's quite another. But the giantess herself was not at all discomposed, either by the introduction or by my rank; and, when I bowed, said, in a voice just like a woman's, "Good-morning, sir; I'm very happy to have the pleasure of making your acquaintance." Mr. Barnum pointed to the sofa by the side of the monster in petticoats, and said; "Do sit down, Sir Lyon;" then, turning to her, "Sir Lyon is a devoted admirer of the ladies." This was more than I had bargained for; but I took the seat, as the best thing to be done under the circumstances.

Miss Condor received Mr. Barnum's remark in regard to my tastes with an enormous simper, and, giantess although she was, turned upon me that indescribable look a woman wears when she is expecting a compliment. I did not know exactly how to pay her one, the circumstances were so very extraordinary, and, I may even say, so embarrassing. So I sat still, and she and Mr. Barnum both looked at me, until it seemed as if I was the show, instead of the giantess. It was beginning to be somewhat oppressive, this interview; yet neither of the other parties seemed to find it so, but looked at me with the utmost serenity, and at each other with no less complaisance.

At last Mr. Barnum said, "Miss Condor, will you be kind enough to rise? Sir Lyon is a great

admirer of the female figure." All this formality
with a giantess that I had expected to see stirred
up like a she bear, considerately, of course,
however! She rose in a dignified and almost
solemn manner; and, as her face ascended, followed by her shoulders, and by her gradually
unfolding drapery, I thought the process of her
elongation would never be accomplished. When
she stood I rose also, it would be hard for me to
tell why; and then, as I contemplated her at an
inconvenient angle, I for the first time realized,
as they say in this country, with what emotions
my friend Petit must look up to Mrs. Petit
(*née* Biggton), who is not only a very supe-
rior woman in the severe style, but also a very
fine woman in the largest style. Under the circumstances, I thought it would be well to pay
Miss Condor the compliment which it would appear that the singular customs of the country lead
giantesses to expect. But while I was thinking
over my subject, and choosing my phrase, Mr.
Barnum suddenly said, "Well, Sir Lyon, I hev
business that calls me away; but don't let that
disturb you. You can remain with Miss Condor
until she is ready to resoome her dooties; and
then " (I assure my readers I am telling them
the truth) "perhaps you'll give her your arm
out!" Saying this, he departed.

I must confess that, admitting Mr. Barnum's
civility in giving me a private view of one of his
curiosities, in the shape the affair was taking, it

did not seem to me at all like the delicate attention on his part that I had been led to expect.
Determining, however, to put the best face upon
the matter, I began a pretty speech; although I
must admit that the combination of vastness and
serenity in my companion's countenance — now
my only companion — was not favorable to
the formation of those dainty and well-turned
phrases with which one likes to placate a lady of
imposing presence. I said, however, that "I was
delighted, in fact quite charmed, to have the
pleasure": — I don't think I got further, or much
further, than that, when the lady sidled toward
me with a movement so tremendous, and beamed
upon me with a smile so expansive, that I must
confess I was somewhat disconcerted, and could
not continue my speech with quite all the coherence and dignity which it is so agreeable for
a man to manifest in presence of one of the other
sex, whatever her condition in life. The consequence was, that I found myself looking up
speechless at this monstrous young woman, who
continued to sidle and simper in her gigantic
fashion. Now, to any one who happens to read
these pages, this may appear a very trifling matter; but that can only be the opinion of men
who have never been placed in my position.
To have a lady pleased with one's company and
with what one says is certainly very gratifying,
especially if the lady herself is an attractive person; but, even in the intercourse of life under

ordinary circumstances, the blandishments which
are so charming in some women are not at all
alluring in others.

I could name many women at home, and have
even seen some in this country, whose gracious
reception of my advances would excite in me
only the liveliest emotions of pleasure; but I must
own that the prospect of becoming the object of
Miss Condor's colossal coquetry produced in me
the most disagreeable sensation of the kind that
I can remember. There I was, quite at her
mercy, as one may say. I candidly confess that
nothing could have been more proper than her
conduct; but I could not but reflect, that, if she
were a designing giantess, my reputation, and
even my purse, was in her power. The situation
was more perilous than that of travelling at home
in a railway carriage with an unprotected female.
What if she should offer to kiss me! I should,
of course, refuse; but would she ravish the sa-
lute? I was but imperfectly acquainted with the
customs here; and above all, I was ignorant of
the manners of giantesses in this strange country.
My thoughts began to come with more rapidity
than coherence, and I decided that the best thing
I could do was to retire. So, after assuring the
lady again that I was delighted to make her acquaintance, and bowing to her as politely as possible, I went quickly out of the room and of the
Museum, determined never again to be left alone
with such a large female of my own species.

CHAPTER V.

AMERICAN MANIA FOR TITLES. — MR. BARNUM AGAIN. — BRIBERY OF MEMBERS OF CONGRESS. — GENERAL SCOTT AND HIS RIVAL. — COURTSHIP AND MARRIAGE IN AMERICA.

THE mania of the Americans for titles is ex- emplified in a remarkable manner by some occurrences of which I have just heard. Mr. Bar- num (whose success is due to his thorough under- standing of the American character), knowing that his countrymen would not take any notice of Tom Thumb unless he had a title, bribed President Pierce and the Senate to appoint him a General in the United States Army. The sum which Mr. Barnum gave the President and each Senator is not exactly known, of course; but I am informed that it was enormous, — so large that since that time these gentlemen, who were men of no fortune before, have kept fast horses, and got drunk upon champagne in the morning, and their wives have worn India shawls and dia- monds to church, thus attaining the chief desires of every male and female American heart. The great showman was of course successful; and the appointment was made, in spite of an indignant remonstrance by General Scott. Mr. Barnum offered to compromise the matter by giving General Scott, who is six feet four inches high, a liberal engagement to appear with his brother General (Tom Thumb), as giant to his dwarf. He thought, he said, that they might play David and Goliath very prettily together, and that the success was sure to be enormous. But this offer General Scott, strange to say (he being only an officer in the United States Army, — a General Lieutenant, or Lieutenant General, or something of the sort, I think they call it), declined to accept in atonement; and the consequence is a lasting coolness between the two rivals. I am even informed that General Scott and General Tom Thumb don't speak.

At present, Mr. Barnum has another dwarf named Nutt, whom he has had made a Commodore in the American Navy, also by bribery of President Lincoln and the Senate; his choice of the navy on this occasion being, not only for the sake of variety, but in compliment to the vigor, efficiency, and consequent popularity of the present head of that Department. Of this fondness of the Americans for titled people I have not yet had any personal experience; but I don't doubt that, as soon as my presence becomes well known in the country, I shall meet with all that deference and attention which an English baronet has the right to expect, and which may possibly make up, in a measure, for other enjoyments that one has at home.

As the marriage ceremonies of foreign and half-civilized people have always been regarded by travellers with great interest, and their accounts of weddings have been read with such avidity by the fair sex in particular, I thought myself fortunate in being in New York at the time when the nuptials of an American General were attracting much attention in what I suppose is the fashionable world of America. I mean, of course, the nuptials of General Tom Thumb, who was married to a female as small as the young woman with whom I had an interview at Mr. Barnum's Museum was enormous. The course of the affair was as follows, as nearly as I can discover.

General Tom Thumb having come to the conclusion that it would be well for him to marry, and having found that the female dwarf's exhibition had been profitable, and that her family were prepared to do well by her, and it being notorious that he had accumulated a pretty fortune, proposals were made on his part, and accepted on hers. It might have been reasonably supposed, that, under such circumstances, there was nothing to be done but for them to be married the next day. Not so, however, among so very singular people as the Americans. Their engagement was announced with some formality. A preliminary ceremony, privately performed, however, was gone through with, called the "presentation of the engagement ring." The lady wore this ring very conspicuously, and much attention was attracted to and much interest manifested in it. Mr. Barnum even announced that she would appear, wearing her "engagement ring," at his Museum. What is still more remarkable, although it was quite well known that the engagement was a business arrangement, the lady and gentleman were congratulated by their friends as if they had each attained a very great happiness; and, stranger than all, they were expected to behave just as if they were in love with each other, like a young man and woman in an English novel. I leave it to those who may read my diary to account for a custom not only so unreasonable, but so at variance with the practice of civilized people.

As the wedding-day approached, all the friends and intimate acquaintances of the lady began to be concerned as to what present they were expected to make to her upon the occasion. For from every such person a present, and one of some value, was looked for by the young woman; and it is even said, that the probable number and value of these presents formed one of the considerations which led both her and her parents to consent to the marriage. This, it will be seen, was quite a semi-barbarous view of the affair; in fact, very much like that which prevails among negroes and Tartars. The presents provided, and the day at hand, there was, on the day previous to the marriage, another strange occur-

rence. This was no other than a rehearsal of
the marriage itself, — an actual dress rehearsal,
such as actors sometimes have of a play the day
before its first performance. I am assured, however, that the marriage rehearsal always stops
with the ceremony; but, if it did not, it is diffi-
cult to see what harm could be done, as the rehearsal includes the clergyman, and would seem
to be quite as binding as that of which it is but
the foreshadow.

The day of the final ceremony having arrived,
presents began to come in; and, as they were
both rich and numerous, the spirits of the bride
and of her mother and her female relatives showed
a corresponding elation. The marriage ceremony
differed in no respect from that of persons in a
similar position in England; and, this briefly over,
the inspection of the wedding presents began,
which, according to the observation of travellers in
all barbarous and half-civilized countries, seemed
to be regarded as by far the most interesting and
important part of the nuptials. These presents
were displayed in the bride's dressing-room and
in the bridal chamber itself. They consisted, not
only of jewels and other like keepsakes, but of
household articles, silver, table furniture of all
kinds, shawls, lace, and rich dresses. Among
the articles exhibited was the night-gear, very
elaborately made, of both bride and bridegroom.
This, I suppose, is done only in compliance with
some rigid religious exaction. But there they

were; the bride's night-gown richly laced, and the bridegroom's night-shirt elaborately ruffled, displayed upon the very bridal bed. I am informed that this singular exhibition was first made in families who hold themselves as of the very highest distinction in the society of this city.

Mr. Barnum, of course, could not let this most interesting occasion pass without turning it to account; and so, as I was informed by an obliging American friend, Jaffier Hokes, he announced that a select company would be admitted "to view the nuptial chamber and couch;" "that the bride would arrive, accompanied by an escort of distinguished matrons," pass into her dressing-room; that "General Tom Thumb would then arrive, attended by quite a number of our most eminent citizens," and pass into the nuptial chamber; and that there, as Mr. Barnum prides himself upon conducting all his exhibitions in a manner "that will not bring a blush upon the cheek of innocence," he "chastely draws a veil which none of the large sums yet offered have tempted him to raise." And there, also, I pause in my description of a marriage in the best society of the most important city in America.

CHAPTER VI.

SUPPER-PARTY IN HONOR OF GENERAL BLUPHER. — SINGULAR
INTRODUCTIONS. — THE EMINENT CITIZENS OF NEW YORK.
— A LARGE MERCHANT. — MASS-MEETING AT SUPPER-TABLE.
— A RISING YOUNG MAN IN WALL STREET. — A NEW AC-
QUAINTANCE.

I WENT last evening to a supper-party given
in honor of Brigadier-General Blupher, by
a Mr. F——, to whom I had letters of credit.
There were no ladies present; but the number
of male guests was so great, that I thought I had
got into one of their "mass-meetings," instead of
a festive gathering. This impression was deep-
ened by the fact, that the evening was passed,
not in sociability, but in political conversation,
and in proceedings.

After guests enough had arrived to make the
crowd sufficiently uncomfortable to gratify the
vanity of the host and his principal guest, the latter was formally presented to the company, and
a speech was made to him, to which he replied in
another, much longer than most of those that are
made in Parliament; and then all the company
filed past him, and were introduced by the host
singly, and had the pleasure of a pull at his arm,

and of being told that he was very happy to make their acquaintance.

I was impressed this evening by the other introductions to which I was a party, and by the manner of their making. Soon after the introduction to General Blupher, which seemed much like taking the ayes and noes in the House, my new acquaintance, Mr. F——, stepped up to me, and, with some earnestness of manner, said, "Sir Lyon, I should like to introduce to you my friend, Mr. G——, of G., H. & Co. He is worth three-quarters of a million of dollars." Of course I said yes; whereupon, *I* was introduced to *him*. I had hardly, however, got over the rough threshold of formal acquaintance, when my host stepped up again, and, interrupting my conversation with Mr. G——, said, under breath, with a serious air, and evidently much impressed, "Sir Lyon, my friend, Mr. K., who realized three millions of dollars in petroleum, — *realized*, — is just yonder. I shall be happy to introduce him. You will see that we have quite a number of our most eminent citizens here this evening." Of course I again assented, and shook hands with the eminent citizen. But I was not able to make conversation go very well with him or with his predecessor. I finally made a little headway by talking to one about wine, and telling the other my opinion as to the certainty of the repudiation of their war debt by the Federals, and so got on with a sort of triangular confab, like Ristori dictating two letters to her two secretaries in "Elizabeth." For, although Mr. G. and Mr. K. had been introduced to me, they had not been introduced to each other, and so could not speak.

I had just got pretty well a-going, and was telling Mr. K. how impossible it was for his government to succeed, and how outrageous its success would be even if it were possible, and how, whether it succeeded or not, such an enormous debt incurred by a people who had never submitted to taxation, and who thought it the finest thing to be what they call "smart," would surely be repudiated in obedience to the dictates of the mob, which would never submit to an income tax, for instance, which we can hardly bear at home (the "Times" expresses my opinion exactly), — when our conversation was interrupted by the sound of my host's voice, saying, with much solemnity, "Sir Lyon, allow me the pleasure of introducing my friend, Mr. L——, the largest merchant in the universe." I turned with a vague expectation of beholding an immense person of the commercial species, when imagine my surprise at seeing a little knock-kneed man, with lead-colored eyes, a sharp nose, a few wandering hairs upon his cheek and chin, and a complexion like sodden pie-crust. The disappointment was the greater, that the two other eminent citizens, who had attained the elevations, respectively, of $750,000 and $3,000,000, were well-grown, robust men, owing, I suppose, to some English blood in their veins.

I saw at once that the idea of largeness was to be connected with my new acquaintance's business, not with his person; and I opened the conversation by saying to my host, "So Mr. L—— is a very large merchant, eh?"—"Oh, immense," Mr. F—— replied. "You would be astonished if you knew the enormity of some of his transactions." My countenance must indeed have expressed my astonishment at this shameless avowal; but my host, evidently mistaking the occasion of my surprise, and regarding it as a tribute to the commercial magnitude of the eminent citizen, went on: "Makes the best note in the street; A, number 1, gilt-edged, and no mistake." The large merchant accepted the compliment with a feeble attempt at graciousness. I asked him if he had lost many of his ships yet, because of the war.

"Don't hev no ships," he said. "We're 'n dry goods; hulsale 'n jobb-in. We do more 't jobb-in 'n any other haouse in the country. Dunno but 'drather job 'n hulsale. Jobb-in's lively; keeps biz-ness mov-in."

And so, after all, this great merchant was no merchant; had no ships; in fact, was not engaged in commerce at all; nothing but a haberdasher, with an overgrown trade. I longed to tell him that this was his proper description, and felt, indeed, that it was my duty to do so; but before I could make up my mind as to the most impressive form of words in which to rebuke him as an impostor, he broke in upon me with —

"Biz-ness lively 'n London when you left, Sir Lyon? Much jobb-in doin'? or do you do most there 't hulsale? Hulsale, I sh'd think; but we do most 't jobb-in. Jobbed a hull invice th' other day. Better 'n t' sell 't off in three or four bills 't hulsale. Makes more frens. Gits people int' yer 'stablishment. Way t' git pop'lar. Nawthin' like pop'larity 'n biz-ness 'r any thin' else."

I was about to say something in reply to this large merchant, being determined to administer my proposed rebuke to his false pretences, when there was a movement of the crowd, which an odor of fried oysters, that had for some time pervaded the house, told me was the beginning of a rush to the supper-table. My new acquaintance looked uneasily away from me a moment, and then, saying, "I'm goin' in for some supper," added hurriedly, "Glad to see you daown 't the store, Sir Lyon; 'll show you a leetle the biggest store on this planet. 'n Miss L. (I found that he meant to say Mrs. L.) 'll be glad to see you 't aour house in Fifth Avenoo. Do come; glad to see yuh, any time." Saying which, he shuffled off with great rapidity into the crowd that was pushing its way in to supper.

While I was gazing after him in some perplexity of mind, I saw my host forcing his way, against the human stream, out of the supper-room. He came toward me somewhat more rapidly than I like to be approached, and said, "Ain't you goin' to take some supper, Sir Lyon? Do allow

me the pleasure of takin' you in." I assented,
and he accompanied me, evidently putting a re-
straint upon his steps, and looking nervously
around him at his guests as he went.

The supper-room was filled as closely as it
could be packed. Men were squeezing past each
other by main force, elbowing their way, treading
upon each other's toes, and painfully working
their passage to and from the table. Some held
their plates against their breasts, others theirs
high in air, like the attendants in pictures of
feasts by the old masters. What most disgusted
me was to see the good nature with which all
this was borne. Each man, instead of showing
any resentment at the way in which he was
crowded, or by word or manner intimating that
the crowd was unpleasant, was smiling and trying
to persuade himself and those who pressed round
him, that he was as comfortable as possible. My
host forced an opening which I entered, but which
immediately closed up around me like water. I
never suffered such severe abdominal compression
in my life; not even when I wore, for a day, Dr.
Stiphstay's medicated instrument for the preven-
tion of an undue development of adipose matter
around the stomach. The perspiration stood in
drops upon my brow, and I felt as if my eyes were
starting from my head. My host, who, I candidly
admit, seemed most hospitably disposed, soon
brought me, although with great difficulty, a plate
of terrapin soup, which seems to be a stew made

of some sort of tortoise, served up, body, bones, and all. It was a black, muddy-looking mess; and, in my squeezed condition, I felt that to introduce any thing within my person that would increase the pressure was not to be thought of. But the union of example with the savory and appetizing steam that came up to my nostrils from the plate overcame both my feeling of discomfort and my prejudices, and, in a few moments, I was enjoying heartily what proved to be a most delicious compound. It must be confessed, that these Americans, although deprived of many inestimable blessings only to be found in England, have certain compensations which are not to be despised. But what may we not expect? Even the Chinaman's bird's-nest soup is said to be a dish of singular delicacy.

After eating one plate of terrapin, I managed to make my way to the table, where I supplied myself with another, which seemed to be even more delightful than the first, especially as it was accompanied with some fine Hock which a dignified colored gentleman pressed upon me with much solemnity. I looked about for an acquaintance to take my wine with; and, not seeing one, I asked a rather niceish but somewhat nondescript-looking person near me to join me in a glass; for, in company, I don't like to drink my wine quite alone. He complied in a very civil kind of way; and we fell into a little chat, in the course of which, I asked him if he could tell me who was

a certain young man around whom a good many
other young men clustered, and who seemed full
of spirits and hilarity.

"Oh! that," said he, "is Jefferson A. Dodger,
one of our most enterprising men in Wall
Street."

"Does a large business, eh ?"

"Oh! very large. Promises soon to become
one of our most eminent citizens."

"What's his business ?"

"Paper."

"Paper in Wall Street! I thought that location,
as you call it here, was given up to money."

"Well, business paper; negotiable paper."

"Ah! I understand; what we call a bill-broker."

"Rather guess not. He don't buy; he always
sells."

"Ah! I see; a capitalist."

"Not much; at least, not yet. Soon will be,
though, if he goes on as he does now."

"I beg pardon; I can't see, exactly. Neither
a bill-broker nor a capitalist, and yet a dealer in
negotiable paper."

"Well, you see," significantly, "he *makes* his
paper. He's got notes for sale, but never buys
any. Always some on hand, with good en-
dorsers. He has quite a talent for making negotiable paper. You understand? It isn't a very
reg'lar business; but the brokers know all about
it, and there's a pleasant mutual understanding
all around."

The light broke in upon me. "What a scoundrel!" I exclaimed.

"No, there you make quite a mistake," said my companion. Jefferson A. Dodger is strictly honorable. Never 's allowed a note to go to protest yet. In fact, some of the brokers say, that they rather prefer buying notes of Dodger, or accepting his collaterals, because, owing to peculiar circumstances, they 'd be sure to be taken care of, whatever happened. So you see, that although, as I said before, business done in that way isn't quite reg'lar, it's as safe as most business, and is *ver-y* profitable. Gives a man a chance, too, to show business talent and enterprise, and to become known as a bold operator. And so long as a man pays his notes punctually and honorably, who has any right to be prying into the way he conducts his business?"

I turned away in mute astonishment. This is commercial honor in the boasted Great Republic! And, will it be believed, I soon saw this same communicative American telling the same story again to others, with even more shamelessness than he had shown in telling it to me. I knew he was going over the same story; for I saw both him and his companion glance at the hero of the tale and at me; and, dreadful to relate, during the horrid recital they laughed as if they were really enjoying a good joke.

But now a bright thought struck me. Here was a most useful acquaintance: communicative, as I had seen, and well-informed about the country I could not doubt. He was just the man for me to cultivate for the sake of the information he was so ready to impart. Soon after, therefore, I approached him, and, thanking him for the interesting explanation he had given me, I begged him to allow me to introduce myself to him, and to solicit the pleasure of his acquaintance, at the same time taking out my card. He was kind enough to say, that he had heard of me before, and knew who I was when I first addressed him, which was very pleasant; as it is always gratifying to find one's self properly appreciated. He added, that he should not have thought of telling Dodger's story to an American. Not necessary to tell it, I suppose; the shameful affair well known. What might I expect from such brigands as those in the omnibus the other day; and from a people who will enter upon the most extravagant war that was ever fought, when their finances are in such a condition that they can't pay the promised seven per cent on my stock! My companionable acquaintance took a card out of his pocket, and, writing his address upon it, handed it to me. It was

JAFFIER HOKES, ESQ.

(Oh! thought I, Americans write themselves down esquires.) He added, that he would soon have the pleasure of calling upon me; that his family were pretty well scattered over the Union;

and that, wherever I went, if I would only produce that card and inform them who I was, I
should be almost sure to find some person as
ready as himself to give me information. We
soon parted, and I did not see him again during
the evening. A very valuable acquaintance, indeed.

CHAPTER VII.

AN AMERICAN TEMPLE. — REFLECTIONS UPON THE AMERICAN
RELIGION. — ANOTHER DISAPPOINTMENT. — THE WAY IN
WHICH AMERICAN WOMEN BUY JEWELS, AND TAKE THEM
HOME. — EFFECT OF DEMOCRACY UPON FEMALE MANNERS.
— THE BOWIE-KNIFE AND ITS USES, SOCIAL AND MERCAN-
TILE.

I WAS surprised this morning to find that they
have a very creditable jeweller's shop here in
the Broadway, very creditable indeed. I candidly admit that I was not displeased at the discovery. In fact, I regarded it, on the whole,
with decided approval, but had, of course, that
shock which one feels at having one's notions of
the fitness of things rudely disturbed. The architecture of the building, and a large clock on
its front, and also the throng of fair devotees
descending from their carriages and pressing
toward its portals, led me at first to suppose it
was a church or American temple. Noticing an
image above the principal entrance, I rejoiced at
the thought of being so soon able, as I thought,
to observe the rites of the real American religion.

I was, of course, aware that various forms of
Protestant Christianity had obtained a foothold in

certain parts of the country; and even that a
variety of the Church of England, the only religion fit for a gentleman, had sprung up somewhere about the States. For Lord Kenyon, with
that munificence peculiarly characteristic of the
British nobleman, had endowed a college here in
the interests of the English Church; how, therefore, could it fail to prosper, that is, in so far as
the instincts of such a people can permit them to
receive with favor so very gentlemanly and thoroughly respectable an institution? But this, and
even the sorts of religion adopted by dissenting
people at home, — for the candid mind cannot
close its eyes to the fact that there are such people
there, — must be regarded as exotic, and quite
incapable of contending here with the Native
American religion proper. This, of course, we
may naturally expect to find a mitigated form of
Paganism; its practices, on the one hand, being
modified by contact with the humanizing influences of Christianity, and its creed and discipline,
on the other, deprived of that latitudinarianism
so widely prevalent among intelligent polythe-
ists by the savage brutality and the intellectual
intolerance which are the distinctive traits of the
American mind. The chief idol must be an em-
bodiment of the deified idea, Majority; and the
bowie-knife is, of course, the official badge and
implement of the priesthood.

Musing thus, I crossed the Broadway, and entered the open door of the supposed temple.

What was my surprise! I found worshippers indeed, and ministrants, nay, sacrifices going on, and all the outward signs of devotion. But it was much what I had seen at home in Regent Street. The worshippers were women; the ministrants, shopmen; the devotion, that undying devotion to dress and trinkets which began with the fall of our race and its exclusion from Paradise; the sacrifices, those inhuman sacrifices of husbands' purses and, sometimes, of women's reputations, which are daily made in London and in Paris. I began to see that civilization had made some progress in America. I again tasted the disappointment of my reasonable expectations, to which I seem to be doomed by the eccentricities of this strange and inconsistent people. Still I was not to be deterred from observation. Noticing that not a few of the ladies present — I suppose that, under the circumstances, it is correct to call them ladies — were apparently of the class to which the young woman belonged whose wiles and false pretences brought upon me my little misadventure the other morning, I determined to purchase something which might smooth my path on another similar occasion, should one arise.

I was making a selection, when a woman entered the shop, and, stepping directly up to the shopman, who was waiting upon me, — quite civilly considering we were in America, — said, "Show me some sets of jewelry, han'some ones." The shopman looked at me with an inquiring and deprecating air; and I, moved by that courtesy so peculiarly English, and wishing also to avail myself of an opportunity of observing the native American of the upper classes, signed to him that he might attend to her.

"What kind shall I show you, madam?" he said. "Dimuns, 'n rubies, 'n emruls, 'n pearls," was the reply. He looked puzzled for a moment, but presently took out a very rich, full set of diamonds, and showed it to her. She was not satisfied; she "guessed she wanted something better 'n that." Her tone was very decided and sharp. She was large and muscular. He then produced, in succession, a set of diamonds and rubies, one of diamonds and emeralds, and a very showy set of pearls.

This seemed more nearly to suit her views, but not to satisfy her. "Let me see somethin' fuss class," she said. "I don't call that fuss class. My husband's in a fuss-class business, an' I want fuss-class jewelry." He smiled deprecatingly, and, after musing for a moment, said, "I'll show you, madam, a necklace and earrings that were made for a Cuban lady of immense wealth, who died before they were finished; so that we took them at a discount, and have them in stock."

Vanishing for a moment, he re-appeared with a large crimson morocco jewel box, lined with purple and gold, from which he took an enormous necklace, in which diamonds, emeralds, rubies, and topazes were profusely mingled; there were huge earrings to match. "Ah! that is fuss class, at last. Why didn't you show me that before? What do you ask for them? But ain't there no teearrer for the head-dress?" Unfortunately, there was not a tiara; and the price was three thousand seven hundred and fifty dollars. She gazed with fascinated eyes a moment, and then said, "There ain't no teearrer, but I'll take 'em.' The shopman bowed, and asked to what address he should send them, and where he should send the bill.

"I'll take 'em with me in my carriage," accenting somewhat the pronoun. "You needn't make no bill. Cash down 's my motto." Saying which, she took out an enormous roll of soiled bank-notes, and counted down seven of five hundred, and two hundred and fifty dollars in smaller notes.

"Will you wait a moment, madam?" said the shopman, moving toward the cashier's desk. "Oh, sartain; see if they 're all right. My husband don't bring me no bogus money, you may bet your life o' that." Then, taking out the earrings she was wearing, she put in those she had just bought. At which I observed the ladies around look at her and at each other in surprise; and a man, evidently belonging to the place, step between her and the door. She, however, was absorbed in her new purchase; and, picking up the necklace, she clasped it around her neck just as the shopman returned, and, bowing to her, said, "All quite right, madam."

"I told you you might bet on it," she said; and, picking up the case, she was about to take it with her. "Let me send it for you, madam." "Well, I don't care if you take it out to my carriage;" and she stalked out of the shop, with all eyes turned upon her.

The shopman returned, and was about to attend to me again, when the lady suddenly re-appeared, and burst in upon us. "Young man, how much 'll it cost to make a teearrer to go 'th that there thing?"—"Indeed, madam, I cannot say just now; but if you'll be kind enough to call to-morrow, I can let you know." —"Very well, I'll call." And she went out again to her carriage; and by the time she was well in it, the whole shop full of people were smiling more or less audibly.

I was much interested and gratified with this exhibition of the debasing effect of democracy upon manners and customs, and of what might be expected in a country which had deprived itself of the benign influences of monarchy, aristocracy, and an established church. Fancy the Duchess of A——, or the Countess of B——, buying a necklace, and walking out of the shop with it upon her neck. I shudder as I think of a Lady Bouse who would be guilty of such an action. What is the much-vaunted elevation of the masses compared with such possibilities?

My mention of the bowie-knife as the insignia of the priesthood of the American religion cannot have surprised the well-informed British reader. Yet this implement is not sacred, or in any way set apart to religious uses. All Americans carry bowie-knives, except Quakers, the editorial staff of the "Tribune," and Henrietta Ward Beecher-Stow, the authoress of "Uncle Tom's Cabin," who preaches here on Plymouth Rock in Brooklyn, and who carries a Sharp's rifle, or a sharp rifle, I don't know exactly which. There is no end to the variety of uses to which the American puts this national implement, — the bowie-knife, — which, I need hardly remind my readers, is merely the scalping-knife and tomahawk of his ancestors, united, enlarged, and brought to a terrible perfection by the cruel arts of American semi-civilization. With it he settles his difficulties, and fights his panics. He trims his nails and cuts his hair with it, — that is, whenever he does trim his nails or cut his hair. Keeping up the custom of his savage forefathers, which compelled each man to carry his own table-furniture, he eats with it; after his meals, he picks his teeth with it; thus, after his fashion, grafting civilization upon barbarism. He also does business with it, and makes it a sort of stock in trade and circulating medium.

I am inclined to doubt the stories told by my predecessors, of two Americans being shut up in a room together, and emerging twenty-four hours after, each with a large fortune made by swapping jack-knives. This, I am quite sure, is a

mere traveller's story, little worthy of credence.
It probably is founded on the fact, that the bowie-
knife, being the only article in the country of
fixed value, is made the basis of all important
financial operations. Thus an American offers
to swap or dicker (an American never says sell
or trade) his bowie-knife with a consignment of
cotton, or a number of shares of bank-stock, to
boot for his correspondent's or business friend's
knife, and certain money, or so much real estate
to boot. The stock or the real estate might fluc-
tuate in value, pending the bargain, as, indeed, I
have discovered to my cost, in case of my own
stock; but the bowie-knife, being in universal
and constant demand, has an absolute, permanent
value; and it must be admitted, that it lends
American trade a certain kind of respectability,
by giving it some sort of metallic basis to rest
upon.

The American, however, finds his bowie-knife
convenient otherwise than as a starting-point of a
negotiation. It has also this importance to him,
that, in case a misunderstanding should occur
between the negotiators, the means are ready at
hand for its satisfactory settlement according to
national custom. Funerals are thus the frequent
consequences of commercial transactions; and a
merchant often contrives to rid himself of a rival
in trade by enticing him into a negotiation. This
he does with perfect impunity. A murder of this
kind is looked upon, like a very large swindle,

only as an interesting and perhaps unfortunate occurrence, which gives the survivor a claim upon public sympathy. As a natural consequence, the phrases, " a sharp bargain," and " on the point of concluding a negotiation," have a peculiar significance in this country, where, indeed, I am inclined to think they had their origin. The bowie-knife thus filling such an important place in business, in amusement, at the table, and the toilet, as well as in war, must be regarded as the most important and characteristic implement of American semi-civilization. I regret to say, that, not having seen one, I am unable to describe it more particularly.